THE GOSPEL OF JESUS CHRIST

According to

JAHZIEL THE FISHER BOY

ROBERT P. BURTON

FOR Additional copies

Robert P. Burton/Bright Morning Star Center for Healing
575 South Street West/Cojean Plaza-Suite #7
Raynham, Massachusetts 02767/#(508) 823-9410
Monday-Saturday 10AM-6PM/EST
<Bmsc2@aol.com> & also place orders @ Amazon.com

THE GOSPEL OF JESUS CHRIST ACCORDING TO
JAHZIEL THE FISHER BOY

TABLE OF CONTENTS

ACKNOWLEDGEMENTS

Thank you to all who had a part in bringing this book together through editing, inspiration, illustration and typing. Without you it may never have come to fruition; Linda Keating, Jean Downey, Karen Burton, Ken Seguin, Melissa Masters and Jolie Matteis.

Jolie Matteis, a mother who resides in Southern California, did the illustrations for this book. Jolie received a two-year degree in Fine Arts at her local community college, then decided to leave school in order to stay home and raise her young son. She now makes and sells crafts from her home where she can be near her child. She was touched to be able to help with the making of this book, as she is also a strong believer in Jesus' message of peace, which will never lose its value no matter how old His story becomes.

FORWARD:

Life continues to offers us daily choices to grow spiritually.

The author of this book, Robert P. Burton, is an excellent role model for what the phrase, "teaching by example", really means.

His willingness to share his knowledge is evident in his every day life including the contents of this book.

Bob attended Great Lakes Bible College in Lansing, Michigan; Johnson Bible College in Knoxville, Tennessee and Bethany Theological Seminary in Dothan, Alabama.

His degrees include a BA in theology, Masters in Pastoral Counseling and Doctor of Biblical Studies.

Other degrees are in Nutrition, American College of Nutrition; Homeopathy, British Institute of Homeopathy; Herbalist, School of Natural Healing and Culinary Arts; Albuquerque Institute of New Mexico.

He is the Pastor for the First Baptist Church of Dighton, Massachusetts and owner of the Bright Morning Star Center for Healing where he offers pastoral counseling.

WHAT'S FOR SUPPER

CHAPTER ONE

"Mother, Mother," yelled the ten-year old Jahziel, a slight, olive-skinned boy with dark brown eyes and shiny black hair, dirty and torn clothes, and worn sandals. "I have seen Him! I have seen Him!," he cried, racing to his home, down the dusty streets of Bethsaida. The boy's mother, at first angry at his absence and presumed irresponsibility, finally took hold of her son, relieved of her worry. She said in a soft voice, "Now, now Jahziel, calm down and tell me where you have been. I found out that your father waited at the dock for his daily food and you never showed up. You've worried us sick and your father has sworn to skin you alive like a fish."

"But mother – the Messiah. He spoke to me and He touched me. I shall never forget it."

"Boy, what are you saying now? Are you trying to call fire down upon our house? Lord forgive him, he is but a child."

"Please, mother, listen. I was headed to the boat to bring father the basket of food you had prepared when I came upon a group of people who were excitedly hurrying along. They were chattering about miracles and the Kingdom of God and freedom for Israel. They seemed so happy, breaking out in spiritual songs and dancing as they went. I was swept along by their joy. I am sorry. I temporarily forgot about bringing father's food to him."

Jahziel went on, "As we left town and started up the mountain, many more groups of people joined with us, all singing and shouting about the same thing.

They were saying the scriptures were being fulfilled before our eyes and that He was the one whom the scriptures spoke of. They said He had raised the dead in Capernaum, healed the lame, and had given sight to the blind. Someone said that He promised the poor a place in the Kingdom of Heaven and warned the scribes and Pharisees that unless they repented of their sins, judgement would be dealt upon them. The stories went on and on, growing more fantastic as we climbed the mountain!"

"Finally, mother, we arrived at a remote place, a large field where many people were sitting about. I made my way through the crowd to the front where I saw this man that they spoke of. He was talking with a dozen or more men, His closest disciples. He looked tired, worn and hungry – like father when he's fished all day on the sea."

"From where I stood, I could hear Him speak, but He spoke not of Himself. He had a voice filled with compassion. He questioned His disciples about the welfare of the people. I heard one say that they didn't have enough money to buy food to satisfy the great number of people gathered. That's when I spotted the kind looking one, Andrew, I think was his name. I approached him and said I wanted to help by donating my food for the people. He took the basket to the to the prophet. That's when I heard Him say, 'Bring the boy to me.' Andrew motioned me over to them. The Holy Man knelt down and asked, 'What is your name boy?' I said, 'Jahziel, son of Shillem of Bethsaida.' He put his hand on my shoulders and said, 'You are anointed by God. Your faith shall save your family. Now stand before Me and hold your basket and you shall see how God will bless your gift.' Then Jesus asked, 'Where is your family, lad?' I said, 'My father is a fisherman and he

is out to sea.' At that point, the Prophet looked out to sea, and with a far away look in His eyes, as if He could see father in the boat, He said, 'Indeed he is, and he is catching many fish.' I tell you, mother, father will come home tonight with a large haul of fish."

"Your father will come home hungry and ready to throw you into the sea," Sari replied.

"No, mother, you must believe me. Listen to what happened next. Messiah instructed the disciples to have the people sit in groups of fifty. There must have been close to twenty thousand people altogether counting men, women and children."

Suddenly, breaking through the heightened emotions of the moment, came an even more chaotic sound. "Sari! Sari!" It was the shrill, high pitched voice of the boy's aunt, his mother's sister, Phoebe. The boy's mother quickly grabbed him by the shoulders and emphatically declared, "Quiet, quiet, not another word of this nonsense! Do not embarrass your family."

As Phoebe entered the house, it was obvious that she was in a state of hysteria proclaiming, "He's here, Sari! He's come!"

"Who, Phoebe, who? Calm down. What are you talking about?"

"The Messiah, Sari! The Prophet, the one called Jesus. He is here in our town, up on the mountain in that area where we used to go for family picnics when we were children. Up where grandfather would tell us stories about the prophets and the promise of the Messiah."

Sari quizzically responded, "Yes, yes, of course I remember. But, if this man were the Messiah, what business would he have on the hillside above Bethsaida?

The prophets tell us the Messiah will be from the city of David and will make Jerusalem His capital. Bethsaida is too far from Jerusalem to be of any importance. Besides, our synagogues are considered second rate. Dear sister, please get a hold of yourself. You're acting like a child with these fantastic stories. This man is just another false prophet looking to get rich off of the poor fishermen. Anyway, if He was the Messiah, He would be in the synagogue with the scribes and Pharisees and the influential. Not up on a hill stealing fish and barley loaves from a naive boy who, incidentally, is in for a rough night when his father gets home. And you, lad, had better have a more truthful story to tell you father." Sari paused and turned toward the door asking, "What is all that noise in the streets?"

Phoebe answered, "It's what I've been trying to tell you about Sari. Listen to the shouts of the people and remember what grandfather often quoted from the prophet about this region, 'The people that walked in darkness have seen a great light. They that dwell in the land of the shadow of death, upon them has the light shined.' "

Looking out the window, Sari gasped as she spoke, "There is no more sunlight in Galilee today as there was in the prophet Isaiah's day!" Just as abruptly she continued, "What are all those people doing out there? Has everyone gone crazy? Am I the only sane person left in Bethsaida? May the Lord be praised! Isn't that Enan, the lame beggar? But, he is dancing and glorifying God. This cannot be!"

While Sari stood momentarily entranced, pondering the meaning of the joyous celebration of the people in the street, the door of the house burst open, as if by a mighty wind. Her wonderment was redirected as Shillem suddenly appeared, passing through the doorway in a ghost-like manner.

Sari, now 32 years of age, had been married to Shillem since she was fourteen. But, she had known him for as long as she could remember because their families were very close. In fact, she and Shillem's sister, Naomi, had been best friends, having grown up in the same neighborhood, sharing the same duties in the synagogue together. But the face of the man she peered into now, could have been that of a stranger. Shillem, somewhat older than she, was a stern, hardworking, serious man. A rugged fisherman, he was more than a little skeptical of the traditional religious practices and the politics of the rulers in the synagogue. This attitude was something Sari and Shillem had in common. She felt she knew her husband better than anyone else knew him. But, this present side of him was totally foreign – a different man. Shillem's face glowed with the child-like innocence of a youngster who had just received a surprise gift. Completely out of character, Shillem began dancing in a circle as he whirled Phoebe around and around. Laughing, he let her go and picked up Jahziel, tossing him in to the air.

Sari, rapidly growing more anxious as she witnessed her typically mundane, sober world instantly transforming into what appeared to be chaos and confusion, began shouting, "Stop! Stop! Tell me what's happening!"

Shillem, still leaping up and down, having taken Sari by the hand while attempting to swing her in circles as he had done with Phoebe, suddenly stopped in his tracks and looked intensely into Sari's eyes. He spoke with a new type of seriousness, one mixed with joy and conviction. He began to unravel the mystery for her saying, "Sari, we are living in truly amazing times. An incredible thing has happened. The long awaited Messiah has arrived. I saw Him. Well, I mean I experienced His presence. We had a very slow day of fishing and it was getting late. We were almost back to shore when I felt what I can only explain as the gaze of the Lord. At first I was frightened, as if I were sinful and had come into the presence of one without sin. It felt like judgement day; it was clearly the presence of God. I think I fell on my face. Then I heard a voice in my head. I know this because no one else on the boat heard this voice. But all were struck with awe, with the presence of the Lord. The voice clearly said, 'Fear not. Arise. Follow Me and I will make you a fisher of men.' I looked around, but there was no one there except for the other men who were all looking at one another in bewilderment. Cousin Samuel said, 'What has happened?' Just then the boat violently shifted to the side as if it was going to sink. We all rushed to our posts in an attempt to keep the boat afloat, when Nathan discovered the problem. The nets were filled to overflowing with fish. With one accord we all praised God as we hauled in the catch. Two miracles in one day – the presence of the Lord and the catching of so many fish! When we arrived at the shore, we were greeted with people singing and dancing. They told us stories of the Messiah and how He healed many people of all kinds of diseases. As a result of today's experience, I feel a personal connection to the Lord. I believe I am suppose to follow Him."

"Sari, I know we have been skeptics of religion in the past. But, this is different. It is as if I know God personally, like Moses experienced. You too shall believe; you will see! For we will meet Him. We will follow Him wherever He leads."

At this point, Jahziel, who knew that speaking out of turn in his father's presence could lead to experiencing his father's heavy hand, could not contain himself. "Forgive me, forgive me father, but I have seen the Messiah. Please let me speak!"

"Father, it was extraordinary. My words cannot do justice to what I felt. Messiah didn't look any different than the common man. But to stand in His presence was unforgettable, like standing before the throne of God. I felt joy and fear together. But, when He spoke to me, an indescribable peace overcame me."

"Yes, yes my son. I felt this same presence on my boat."

"But father, you should have seen what He did with your fish and barley loaves. Jesus took them and, as He looked heavenward, He held them up and prayed, 'Father, as I lift up these loaves and fish before You, so will You lift up the Son of Man that all who believe will be filled with eternal life. Multiply this food to fill all who are here today and let them witness Your great and mighty power and know that the Son has come in Your name.' "

"The Master then began to hand bread and fish to the disciples, who, in turn, distributed it to the many people who were seated there. While the people ate until their stomachs were content, Messiah knelt down and talked with me saying, 'Jahziel, you are a chosen one, chosen by God. You and your family shall follow Me. And you shall see the Son of Man lifted up for the healing of sin, just as Moses lifted up the serpent in the wilderness. After that, you will fall into despair for a short time. Then the Son of Man will appear again and you will see Him ascend into the heavens to the glory of God. Later, you will witness a great miracle of God at the coming of the Holy Spirit. The Spirit will lead your father to Damascus where you shall prepare the way for the coming of one of my messengers. You shall be a scribe, you and your sons, and your sons' sons. You shall preserve the New Covenant for the generations to come, for those living in the last days. Now Jahziel, you must go home and tell your family all that you have seen and heard. But first, here are the fish and loaves you came with. Eat and take the rest home.' "

"Father, I immediately ate two small loaves and one fish because I was so hungry, having not eaten all day. Then, coming down the mountain I ate two more loaves of barley, and look, there are still five loaves and two fish! Father, as I stood next to Jesus when He distributed the loaves and fish, it was like being with God at the time of creation. For He created those loaves and fish out of nothing. Surely He is divine!"

Sari, falling on her knees, arms outstretched toward the heavens, cried out, "God have mercy on me for I did not believe, but now I do. I see in the faces of my husband and son that they have come into the presence of your Son."

Shillem, Jahziel, and Phoebe ran to Sari, embracing her and shouting and laughing for joy.

Jahziel said, "Come! We must find the Messiah and follow Him." But, Shillem overruled the boy stating, "It is night now. The sun has gone down. We must wait until morning. Sari, Phoebe, prepare for the journey. We don't know how long we will be gone. Come son, let us pray and get to bed. There is much work for us to do."

QUESTIONS FOR CHAPTER ONE

"WHAT'S FOR SUPPER"

1. Why did Jahziel forget to bring food to his father?

2. What did Jahziel do with the food?

3. How did Jahziel's father catch so many fish?

4. What did Jesus tell Jahziel about being chosen?

THE BOY WHO FISHED FOR MEN

CHAPTER TWO

"Jahziel, wake up," Sari exclaimed, "everyone has rolled over you and the cock has crowed twice. We'll never catch up with the Messiah moving like a turtle on a log at high noon. Aunt Phoebe and I have packed bread for the journey and we'll buy figs along the way."

As the family set out, a young boy named Nathan, the son of Jacob, a fisherman, and cousin to Jahziel, ran past them shouting, "Everyone's headed to Capernaum. They think Messiah may be headed in that direction." Turning the corner of their street, the family saw many of their neighbors walking westward toward the road to Capernaum. Father said, "Quick, let us go to the docks. We'll take a boat. It will be quicker than walking."

Once they reached the water's edge, they beheld large numbers of fishermen and their families preparing to set out to sea. Everyone was talking about the Messiah and sailing to Capernaum. Singing Psalms and folks songs about the Messiah and Kingdom of God on earth, with Israel as its center, and Jerusalem, the capital of the world, seemed to be the energy that propelled a myriad of tiny wooden fishing boats across the Sea of Galilee toward Capernaum.

Disputes broke out here and there along the shore at Capernaum as fishermen competed for a spot to tie down their boats in an already crowded area. The family of Shillem gathered together on the shore. They checked their food and supplies. Then, after getting directions, the family set off to find the synagogue of Capernaum.

Entering the synagogue, Jahziel spotted the Messiah. He and the Master's eyes met, and with a smile, Jesus motioned for Jahziel and his family to join Him. Making their way through the crowd, the family came before the Lord. Reaching down, Jesus bent over, picking up the boy as He proclaimed, "Ah, Jahziel, my scribe, how are you?" Sari looked to Shillem and quietly said, "Scribe? What can He mean? The boy hardly knows letters." Phoebe whispered, "He's a prophet!"

Riding higher in the arms of Jesus, Jahziel exclaimed, "Rabbi, this is my family. My father, Shillem, my mother, Sari, and my aunt, Phoebe." Jesus greeted them with a hardy "Shalom" and invited the family to sit among the disciples. Then, with Jahziel still held in His arms, Jesus addressed the people gathered in the synagogue, "There shall come forth a rod from the stem of Jesse, and a branch shall grow out of his roots. The Spirit of the Lord shall rest upon Him, the spirit of wisdom and understanding, the spirit of counsel and might, and the spirit of knowledge and of the fear of the Lord. His delight is in the fear of the Lord, and he shall not judge by the sight of his eyes, nor decide by the hearing of his ears. But with righteousness he shall judge the poor, and decide with equity for the meek of the earth; he shall strike the earth with the rod of his mouth, and with the breath of his lips he shall slay the wicked. Righteousness shall be the belt of loins, and faithfulness, the belt of his waist. The wolf also shall dwell with the lamb, the leopard shall lie down with the young goat, the calf and the young lion and the fatling together; and a little child shall lead them."

Many from the crowd knew He had quoted Isaiah and that His reference was to the coming Messiah. But because he held Jahziel in his arms they assumed he was insinuating that Jahziel was the Messiah. Some suggested Jesus must be Elijah if the boy was indeed the Messiah. Others protested, "No, John, the one who baptized us in the Jordan, was Elijah. This man is Messiah but he wants us to listen to the young boy." A great amount of debate broke out among the crowd.

Just about that time, the group who had walked to Capernaum arrived at the synagogue. One of the late arrivals shouted, "Rabbi, when did you come here?" Gently placing Jahziel down at His feet, Jesus looked intently into the crowd and said, "Most assuredly, I say to you, you seek me not because you saw the Son, but because you ate of the loaves and were filled. Do not labor for the food which perishes, but for the food which endures to everlasting life, which the Son of Man will give you, because God the Father has set His seal on Him."

From there the crowd attempted to get Jesus to perform miracles and give them more free food. But Jesus knew that this crowd from the mountainside only wanted Him for personal gain and as an entertainment. Jesus, therefore, spoke to them in parables, at which they walked away from Him and never returned to His ministry.

Anxiously, Jahziel pulled on the robe of Jesus, crying out, "Master, Master, don't let them go. They must understand who you are or they will perish." Shillem grabbed his boy and pulled him close. Then Shillem, with his head bowed before Jesus in humility spoke. "Master, forgive the boy, he doesn't know what he is saying." Crouching down on one knee and looking straight into Jahziel's eyes, Jesus first addressed Shillem. "Yes, the boy does understand, for he will catch more men with the Word of God than all the fish caught by the fishermen of Bethsaida." Then

Jesus spoke quietly to the lad, "Jahziel, do not worry. To all who desire truth, the Spirit will open their hearts. Truly there are some of us who can not hear now, but later their ears will be opened. There are some who are blind but will see. And yes, there are some whose hearts will remain hard forever. They have chosen the path of Egypt's Pharaoh during Moses' day. The more the Lord called to the Pharaoh, the colder and harder his heart grew. But now, my son, you will be my herald. I must go on a journey for a short time. You and your family will go back to Bethsaida and will wait there for me. There is a blind man sitting on a rock outside of the village. You are to go to him every day, bring him food, and tell him the scripture that you have learned. In this way you will prepare his heart so that when I come to Bethsaida, I can heal him."

Jesus then stood up and spoke to Shillem. "Take your family and go back to Bethsaida. Allow the boy to do as I have instructed. You must fish and wait for my return. I am off to Tyre and then Decapolis. After that I will come for you. Go in peace."

QUESTIONS FOR CHAPTER TWO

"THE BOY WHO FISHED FOR MEN"

1.   Do you remember what Jesus asked Jahziel to do for the blind man and where he would find him sitting?

STANDING ON THE ROCK

CHAPTER THREE

Before even the anchor could be cast, Jahziel jumped overboard into the water, swimming as fast as he could toward shore. Shillem, with a loud, deep voice, shouted, "Boy, where are you going? Help us secure the boat." Jahziel shouted back over his shoulder, "Father, I must find the blind man." Phoebe chimed, "Go Jahziel, go!" As soon as Jahziel's feet stepped on dry ground, he was off and running with the speed of the wind. Jahziel found his way through the dusty streets to the main gate of Bethsaida. He ran past the elders and tax collectors and a group of people conducting business with the elders. Jahziel ran down the road past the beggars until suddenly he stopped in his tracks. Breathing heavy and sweating, he stood stunned by the sight before him. Sitting on a rock was a ragged, dusty, hungry looking blind man just as the Messiah had prophesied.

"Food, food," Jahziel whispered to himself. Jesus has said to bring food to the blind man. "I must get some food." The young boy turned in his tracks and ran back past the beggars and elders and others at the main gate. He continued racing past everyone on the main street that ran through the village as anxious thoughts traveling through his mind faster than his legs were moving.

Amazingly, and to Jahaiel's most pleasant surprise, he spied his father's cousin, Esther, walking just ahead of him. Jahziel startled the workman as he grabbed hold of her arm and yanked up and down on Esther's sleeve repeatedly yelling, "Bread! I need bread for the blind man!" In her half shocked state, Esther quickly unfolded a cloth, revealing several small barley loaves. Jahziel snatched

two loaves exclaiming, "Thank you, praise God, thank you!" As the excited lad dashed off down the road, Esther stared after him, shaking her head and quietly saying, "What is Shillem going to do with this mischievous boy?"

Slowing down, his gallop turned to a walk a few feet away from the blind man. Jahziel blurted out, "Sir, I have some barley loaves for you." Turning in the direction of Jahziel's voice and reaching out, the blind man said, "Praise God, thank you Lord." As the blind man gobbled up the tiny loaves, Jahziel excitedly asked. "Do you know Jesus? Have you met the Messiah?" In a sad tone the blind man replied, "No, but I have heard of Him from the people passing by in both directions. First from those going up to the mountain and then from those going to Capernaum to see Him. But Messiah has never passed by Himself. He must travel by boat. No one was willing to lead me by the hand to meet Jesus. I have prayed all my life that I could see the Messiah before I die. But, how foolish is my prayer since I'm just a poor blind man. I wonder what sin my parents must have committed that I was born blind."

Speaking anxiously and rapidly, Jahziel assured the blind man, "Messiah wants to meet you. He told me so when I was in Capernaum. He told me to bring food to you each day until He comes." "Boy, boy," pleaded the blind man, "Why do you harass a poor old blind man? What would Messiah want with me? How would He know who I am?" "Please sir, believe me," Jahziel cried out, "Messiah knows everyone and knows our needs. He loves everyone and His eyes beam with the love of God. You will believe He will come for you. I must get home, but I will be back tomorrow with some bread for you."

Indeed, Jahziel remained true to his word as he returned to feed the blind man day after day. Jahziel learned the blind man's name was Michiah. He was born in Capernaum but had relatives in Bethsaida. Unfortunately, the relatives were poor and could not provide for the blind man so he had to resort to begging.

About thirty days later, Jahziel and Michiah sat eating bread and talking as they did every day. Michiah paused in mid-sentence, sitting straight up and tilting his head to one side as if attempting to listen to some distant sound. Michiah said, "Listen boy, do you hear that? Down by the sea there is a great disturbance, people shouting." "No, I don't hear anything." Jahziel responded. But Michiah insisted that the sound was growing louder and closer. Before long, a crowd was making its way through the main gate from inside the village. People were singing and dancing, shouting, "Messiah has come back to our village!"

Jahziel leaped from the rock and darted toward the crowd cutting into the pack of jubilant devotees. Soon after disappearing into the human amoeba, the crowd opened up and Jahziel appeared, leading the Messiah by the hand. The boy was shouting, "Michiah, Michiah. The Messiah is here just like I promised." The crowd encircled the rock with the blind man sitting upon it looking bewildered. As Jesus raised His hand the crowd became as silent as the wilderness at night. Jesus quietly spoke the name of the blind beggar, "Michiah." From his throne of stone, the poor man joyfully replied, "My ears have heard the sound of my Savior, now I beg you, allow my eyes to see His glory." With that, Jesus lowered His hand, gently passing it over Michiah's face and saying, "So be it, your faith has healed you." As Michiah's eyes opened, he exclaimed, "Who is like Jehovah, my Lord and my God."

Jesus climbed to the top of the rock and then, reaching down, He gently lifted

Jahziel up to Himself. Standing atop the rock with His arms around the shoulders of the boy and Michiah, the Messiah spoke to the crowd that surrounded the rock. "Surely, today light has come to a people living in darkness by the sea. But do you know where the light comes from? Do you know the bearer of this light and His purpose? Today a blind man receives his sight, but it is with his soul he now sees the truth. I tell you, it is better for a man to have never seen the world around him and yet know the truth than to have seen the wonders of the world and yet, his soul lives in darkness."

"God is the source of true light," Jesus went on. "He has sent His Son to bring light into the world but the heart of man is evil. Many will turn from the light and will treat the Son in the same manner that their fathers treated the prophets of old. But, a remnant will be saved."

"The Kingdom of God is like a landowner who set up his fields and hired men to care for his crops. Then the landowner went away, and when it was time for the harvest, he sent a servant to collect his due. The hired workers beat the servant and chased him away. The landowner sent two more servants but they were treated in the same manner. Finally, the landowner sent his only son, thinking, 'surely they will respect my son.' But the hired men killed the landowner's son and said, 'Now we will keep all the profits for ourselves.' What do you think the landowner will do to those evil workers when he returns with his army?"

After this, Jesus got down from the rock along with Jahziel and Michiah. As the crowd murmured among themselves concerning the meaning of the parable, Jesus quietly gave instructions to Jahziel and Michiah. Jesus said, "Jahziel, take

Michiah to your father and tell him I said to train Michiah to take over the fishing business. I must go away again, but when I return, you and your family must accompany me for you will eventually witness the Son of Man lifted up."

After saying this, Jesus and his disciples seemed to vanish through the crowd. While Jahziel and Michiah stood there amazed at what had just happened, someone in the crowd shouted, "Where is Jesus?" The crowd began to disperse into different directions, each group going in the direction they thought Jesus had gone. Jahziel would later learn that Jesus took Peter, James and John to the top of Mount Herman where He revealed His glory to them. It was said that Jesus' face shined with such intensity that it caused the three disciples faces to shine also.

The boy and his once blind friend walked to the dock to wait for Shillem. When they reached the water's edge, Michiah said, "I see a boat coming this way." He then began to praise God saying, "Yes, I see, thank you Lord!" The boy walked out toward the boat to help with securing it.

QUESTIONS FOR CHAPTER THREE

"STANDING ON THE ROCK"

1. Can you recall what the blind man had prayed for all of his life?

2. How did Jesus help the blind man?

3. When Jesus left the area, He and some of His disciples went up to Mount Herman. Can you describe what happened to Jesus' face?

GOD LOVES THE LITTLE CHILDREN

CHAPTER FOUR

Ten days passed since Michiah had been healed of blindness. Every day Jahziel wondered if Jesus would return that day. The men were out on the sea trolling for fish when a strong wind rose up and drove the boat toward Capernaum. When the wind stopped and the boat came to rest in the Bay of Capernaum, Shillem noticed the boat tilted to one side. He jumped out into the water to check the hull for damage. To Shillem's pleasant surprise, he discovered the boat's leaning was due to the nets being filled with fish. Immediately, he remembered the miracle the Lord had previously performed. An excited Shillem called to the crews, "The Lord is near." He decided to take their catch, bring it to Capernaum and sell it there.

After taking care of business, Shillem said that he felt the Lord might be in Capernaum. The crew stayed with the boat and Shillem, Jahziel, and Michiah walked in the direction of the synagogue where Jesus had previously taught when he was in town. Along the road they met some people who told them that Jesus was at Peter's mother-in-law's house.

Outside the door of the house a woman named Tabetha greeted them. She said Jesus had been expecting them. When she brought them to Jesus, His first words were, "You showed great faith during the storm." Shillem and Michiah looked at each other with facial expressions that said, "How did He know?" Jahziel just smiled.

Jesus turned to Michiah and told him that in the morning he was to return with the crew to Bethsaida and he was to take care of the family while Shillem and Jahziel would travel with Jesus. Then Jesus took Jahziel and sat him on His lap and spoke to those sitting around him, "See that you do not look down on one of these little ones for I tell you that their angels in heaven always see the face of my Father."

Shillem pondered this teaching, it confirmed what he had believed, that there are guardian angels watching over people. Jesus' teaching further taught that the guardian angels of little children hold a special place with God the Father. It appears that their angels must be positioned very close to the throne of God as Jesus stated, "They see the face of God." What a wonderful lesson for the children to know that God loves them so dearly. They can feel safe that their personal angels and God are looking out for them. Shillem was pleased in believing his son, Jahziel, would be safe with the Lord.

That day in the house, Jesus spoke several parables, but the one Jahziel remembered the most was about a shepherd who left ninety-nine sheep on a hill while he went to look for the one that was lost. Jahziel realized that everyone is important and loved by God. The young boy also made a promise to God that he, too, would accept everyone as equal and never forsake those who might be treated as less important, or may wander from the group.

Michiah also learned a valuable lesson that day. Jesus told a parable about an unmerciful servant who was treated kindly by the king but had no mercy on someone who owed him a small amount of money. Michiah thought about how kind God was in healing him and how God gave him the opportunity to take over the fishing boat and live with Shillem's family. Michiah vowed that day to always be merciful toward others.

After the evening meal, as the followers were preparing for bed, Jahziel overheard Peter and John talking about what they had seen when they were up on the mountain with Jesus after leaving Bathsaida. Peter said that Jesus' face shined in the way that Moses' face had shined when Moses had been up on the mountain with God. John replied, "What about the voice we heard? Was that not the voice of God?" "Yes, yes," Said Peter. "I tell you, this proves Jesus is the Messiah." Just then James came over and said, "Keep your voices down, don't you remember what the Lord told us? We are not to let this out until the Son of Man is raised from the dead." Peter whispered, "What did He mean by that remark, raised from the dead?... We should ask Him."

When everyone was settled in bed, Jahziel found it difficult to fall asleep. As he lay there between Shillem and Michiah, Jahziel thought about the events of the day. Just before falling to sleep, a feeling of sadness momentarily came over the boy as he remembered this would be his first night away from his mother, and certainly he would miss Michiah who had become a family member. But, of course, traveling with Jesus and the disciples, plus having his father with him, would be an exciting time. As he drifted off to sleep, Jahziel prayed, "Thank you God for your love and for your angels."

QUESTIONS FOR CHAPTER FOUR

"GOD LOVES THE LITTLE CHILDREN"

1.   What did Jahziel learn from the parable that Jesus taught about the one lost sheep?

2.   What did Michiah learn from the parable about the unmerciful servant?

WRITING LOVE LETTERS IN THE SAND

CHAPTER FIVE

Cock-a-doodle-do, the cock crowed for the third time. Peter sat straight up with a startled look on his face. "What's the problem Peter?" James asked. Peter sleepily replied, "I don't know, I had a strange dream. In my dream I saw the Lord standing at a distance with a lonely and sad expression on His face, and I was repeating over and over again, 'I don't know Him.' " "Oh Peter," said James, "Your head is filled with too much sea water. You would never do anything like that! Stop with the fish stories."

Shillem bellowed out, "Where is my boy?" James replied, "He's gone with Jesus. The Lord likes to walk quietly and contemplate in the morning. I'm sure the boy will learn a valuable lesson. The Master has taken a special interest in this boy; you should be proud."

Jesus gently spoke to Jahziel, "It is a beautiful morning here by the Sea of Galilee, Jahziel. Whenever I'm in Capernaum I walk along this shore in the early morning. I come here to talk with my Father." Jahziel quizzically responded, "But Jesus, there is only you and me here. Where is your Father?"

"My Father is present everywhere." Jesus answered.

"What do you mean, present everywhere? Please Master, explain to me. I want to know what this means."

"Well son, do you know that God is a spirit?"

"Yes Master, I know this."

"Now understand lad, God is not limited, like created beings, as to how time and space exits. A human being is bound by the laws of God's creation. You can not be in more than one place at a time."

"Yes, I know Master."

Jesus went on, "You may not be able to understand this, but think of God as being so large that He can fill every space inside and outside of the created world, even though you cannot see Him."

"I think I understand Master," said Jahziel, "God is like a giant ghost."

"That will be have to be sufficient for now, my son." Jesus replied.

"Master, when you talk to God, do you mean you recite the prayers that we are taught in synagogue?"

"Your question is beyond your years lad, but it is a good one. The prayers you learned in synagogue and the ones your parents have taught are good prayers. Those prayers were the prayers of our ancestors, Moses, David, Solomon, and others. They were the words of their hearts and they teach us of the history of God's people and help us to understand the heart of the Father. But, my son, God wants to hear from your heart. Prayer can help you learn not only about God, but also about yourself. When we pray from our heart, it helps us to hear our own needs and to realize how much we need the help of God. Jahziel, I want you to write down your prayers so that you can look back and see how God has answered your prayers and how He helped you to grow up and overcome the difficulties of life."

"Yes Master, I believe you are correct. Looking back on my prayers would show me how God has helped me. But, you must know that I have not yet learned letters," Jahziel confessed.

Jesus smiled and He knelt down facing the boy. "Jahziel, do you remember that I said you will be my scribe?"

"Yes Master, but when?"

Jesus spoke softly, "Do you have faith in my Father?"

"Yes Jesus," said the boy.

"Then you also have faith in Me."

"Yes Master."

Jesus then instructed the boy, "Ask my Father to grant you the gift of letters. Place your hand in mine." Both Jesus and Jahziel bowed their heads. Jahziel tightened his grip on Jesus and quietly yet confidently prayed. "Heavenly Father, you are most holy. Please forgive my sins. I try hard to obey my parents but sometimes I forget the rules. Your Son, Jesus, wants me to be His scribe but I have never learned to write. I believe you have power over your creation, so please give me this special gift. Thank you."

Jesus and Jahziel looked at each other face to face and Jesus said, "Do you believe it has taken place?"

"Yes Master," replied Jahziel.

"Look out into the Sea of Galilee. What do you see Jahziel?"

"I see boats."

"Tell me lad, how do the boats move?"

"By the wind, Master."

"Yes, Jahziel, by the force of the wind and by the waves."

"Yes, Master."

"Listen carefully boy. Sometimes the wind and the waves become so strong that the little boats are tossed about out of the control of the fishermen and their lives become endangered."

"Yes, this is true Master. I have experienced this," said Jahziel.

Jesus continued, "The boat is like our faith. If we have great faith, our lives like the boat, sail smoothly. But if we doubt, then we are tossed to and fro like the boat in the storm. Do you understand, boy?"

"Yes Master, I have faith."

"Then sit here and write in the sand, Jahziel."

The boy squatted down and wrote, "Blessed is he who lives by faith and does not doubt." He then exclaimed, "Jesus, look at my letters!"

"Yes Jahziel, your faith is strong. But remember this: your Father in heaven has chosen you to be my scribe and has given you this gift as a sign to you that I am He who takes away the sin of the world, and I must die and be raised up on the third day. You are to tell my story and to write my words on a scroll. Not everything you pray for will come this easily. Sometimes the Father requires the believer to walk by faith through the fire. Our struggles teach us much, if we endure in faith," explained Jesus.

"Jahziel, do you know the story about Jacob, Leah and Rachel?"

"Yes Master, I know it well. My father has told it to me many times."

"Well then Jahziel, tell it to me as you understand it."

"But Master, you are the teacher. How can I teach you?"

"Let it be for now, Jahziel."

"Well Master, this is how it goes. Jacob wanted to marry Rachel, and so he went to her father, Laban, and asked for permission to marry her. Laban told Jacob he must first work for him for seven years, then he would receive permission to marry Laban's daughter. Jacob agreed, and for every day for seven years, as Jacob worked hard, his love for Rachel grew. At the end of the seven years Laban informed Jacob that according to local custom, the oldest daughter must marry first. Leah was the oldest, and so Jacob had to marry her and work another seven years before he could marry Rachel. This is the story Master," said Jahziel.

"And what is the lesson you learn from this story of your ancestors?"

Jahziel thought for a moment, then said, "Fourteen years, Jacob waited fourteen years to marry Rachel. He must have loved her very much."

"Yes Jahziel, Jacob did love her, but wasn't that a long time to wait?"

"Yes Master, but if it's something we really want, it is worth it," the boy replied. Jesus prompted him, "What does the story tell you about prayer?"

Jahziel thought again, then said, "If we ask for something, the answer does not always come quickly. Sometimes we will wait for a long time, but it is worth it."

"Yes my son, you learn well. You have received a gift from God today, but don't expect everything to be that easy. Come Jahziel, the sun is rising and I hear the sound of footsteps approaching."

QUESTIONS FOR CHAPTER FIVE

"WRITING LOVE LETTERS IN THE SAND"

1.   Please explain why writing down our prayers can help us later in life.

2.   Try to describe how a boat is like faith as Jesus taught.

3.   Discuss the lesson Jesus gave Jahziel involving waiting for our prayers to be answered.

THE SEED THAT GREW INTO A KINGDOM

CHAPTER SIX

As the bright morning sun began to show its face upon the horizon of the calm Sea of Galilee, Jesus and Jahziel strolled along the sands, hand in hand. Jahziel felt a warm calm peace in his heart. Suddenly, the sharp sound of a woman's voice came piercing through the morning quiet, "Master, Master, there you are. Wait for us." It was Joanna, followed by Susanna and Mary, along with the disciples and Shillem. Soon, many others from the towns and villages around Galilee arrived, wanting to hear Jesus speak and demanding miracles of Him.

Jesus scooped up Jahziel and waded to a boat belonging to Zebedee, the father of the disciples James and John. Climbing in, Jesus and Jahziel sat down. James, John, Andrew and Phillip, led by Peter, waded out and encircled the boat, preventing anyone else from crowding the Master. As Jesus looked beyond the crowd of people on the beach, to the hillside, He saw a farmer sowing seeds. Jahziel noticed a far away and deeply sad expression on the Master's face.

Jesus then looked right into Jahziel's eyes and said, "Listen and heed! A farmer went out to sow his seed. As he was scattering the seed, some fell along the path and birds came and ate it up. Some fell on rocky places where there wasn't much soil. It sprang up quickly because the soil was shallow. But, when the sun came up, the plants were scorched and they withered because they had no water. Other seed fell on good soil. It came up, grew and produced a crop, multiplying thirty, sixty, or even a hundred times." Then, looking at the crowd, Jesus said, "He who has ears, let him hear."

The crowd on the beach began to discuss among themselves the meaning of the parable. Peter spoke up and said, "Lord, tell us the meaning of the parable." Jesus thought for a moment and then He said to Jahziel, "Tell us, how does the farmer spread his seed?" The young boy replied, "Well, as you know my father is a fisherman, but I do have an uncle who farms over by Bethsaida. On occasion I have accompanied him. Uncle walks along the paths that cut through his fields. He carries a large burlap bag over his shoulder. The bag is filled with flaxseeds. As he walks along the earth, he reaches in and takes a handful of seeds. Then he tosses them toward the center of the field where the soil is rich. Some of those seeds fall on the ground by my uncle's feet. They get stepped on and never grow. Also, there is a border of rocks around the field and that is not a good place for seeds to grow. Then there are thorns near the edge of a field and they do not allow the plants to grow very well. But, the rest of the field is rich soil and the seeds that make it there usually yield tall, healthy flax."

"Yes Jahziel, you are very observant," replied Jesus. "But what does the seed represent?" The disciples muttered among themselves, then Jahziel blurted out, "Your words Master! The seeds are a symbol of the things you teach us about the kingdom." "Very good my son," said Jesus, "and when someone does not embrace it immediately, the devil comes and snatches away what was sown in the heart. This is the seed that falls on the path and is trampled by people's feet."

"Master, is this why you often look sad when there is a great crowd around you? Because you know that some will not listen?" Jesus gently smiled upon the

boy. Then He continued, "As to the seed that fell on rocky ground, it is like the person who hears the message of salvation and believes it, but when trouble comes, he quickly falls away because he is not seriously committed to following God. It is very important that we learn as much as we can about God so we can defend our belief."

"Now, about the seed that fell among the thorns. This is similar to the person who hears the message but is more concerned with being rich and having luxuries. He places all his energy into gaining wealth and doesn't pay any attention to God."

"Finally," Jesus went on, "there is the one who receives the message of salvation, believes it, takes it seriously, and lives for God. This person will tell others about the message of salvation but will also learn to be kind and gentle and help other people."

Jahziel had an excited look on his face as if he had just come to understand something very important. "Master, I am like the seed that fell on rich soil. I believe you are the Messiah who has come to save our souls. And I want to share the message with others so they can come to have eternal life also. Master, please, baptize me into your kingdom."

Jesus said to Jahziel, "Your heart is pure and I will baptize you. Come, let's get into the water." Jesus jumped out of the side of the boat and stood in waist deep water between Peter and Shillem. The boy climbed onto Jesus' shoulders. Jesus turned and walked back toward the shore where the water was not so deep. He set Jahziel down in the water just above the boy's waist. Jesus placed one hand behind Jahziel's head and with the other hand He gripped both of Jahziel's wrists. At that, Jesus said, "Jahziel, you will witness many miracles and proofs of the Son of Man. You will write them for many others to believe. And wherever you go, whenever your words are read, children will believe. This day I baptize you into repentance and eternal life in the name of the Father, the Son and the Holy Spirit."

Jesus then gently guided Jahziel beneath the water and up again. When Jahziel came up out of the water, he felt a quiet, still, peacefulness inside and all around him as if he was standing alone in the presence of God and God was very pleased with him. Jahziel also felt a new strength, desire and confidence to tell everyone about Jesus. Just then, Jahziel saw throngs of people from the shore rushing into the water and shouting out for Jesus to baptize them. Hundreds were baptized that day, but of the many, Jahziel remembered the first one baptized after him – his father, Shillem. He remembered the words of Jesus addressed to his father, "Watch over this boy for I will soon go to the Father and my scribe will bring light into the darkness."

QUESTIONS FOR CHAPTER SIX

"THE SEED THAT GREW INTO A KINGDOM"

1.   What did Jahziel tell Jesus about being a seed that fell on rich soil?

2.   Please describe how Jahziel felt after being baptized.

A VISIT TO GOD'S HOUSE

CHAPTER SEVEN

The road was cluttered with stones and rocks, making it difficult to walk. The heat of the September sun beat on Jahziel's head. He was growing hungry and weary from walking all day with Jesus. Jesus seemed to be in more of a quiet mood as he hadn't said much to the boy all day. Jahziel knew they were headed for Jerusalem because Jesus had sent Shillem, the disciples, and others ahead to the city. Finally, the boy broke the silence, "Master, tell me about Jerusalem and the festival we are going to."

"Well Jahziel, first of all, Jerusalem is also called the city of God. It sits high on a mountain top. That is why we say we are going 'up' to Jerusalem. It is said to be God's favorite spot on earth, but I know of a garden far away that God loves equally. Jerusalem is a beautiful city with high walls all around it and there are twelve gates by which to enter, but enough about the physical beauty of the city. What truly makes it beautiful is its holiness. The temple of God is on that holy mountain and seven times a year there are festivals appointed by God. The one we will be attending shortly is the feast of tabernacles, or booths, sometimes simply called 'the feast' "

"Yes Master, I know this festival," shouted Jahziel, "we celebrate this every year in my town. We are required to leave our homes and live temporarily in shelters that we make ourselves. It is an exciting time."

"True," said Jesus, "but you do you know the meaning of living in the booths, Jahziel?"

"I do. We stay in these crude shelters for a week to remind ourselves of how God brought our ancestors through the wilderness after bringing them out of slavery in Egypt."

"Very good Jahziel!" And when we get to Jerusalem, you will see thousands camped out in little huts made of palm branches and brush. Every day the people will follow a priest down to the pool of Siloam where he will fill a golden pitcher with water. Then the people will follow the priest back to the temple. Everyone will recite scripture and sing psalms. Then the priest will pour out the water as an offering to God, and the people will wave palm branches and shout, 'Oh give thanks to the Lord!' And, on the last day of the feast, we will march in a circle, shouting and praising God in remembrance of the first victory in Israel. Do you remember what that victory was, Jahziel?"

"Yes Master. It was Jericho when the walls fell down."

"Ah, yes Jahziel. You have been taught well."

When Jesus and Jahziel came up the mountainside, the great walls of Jerusalem, the Holy City, came into view. Entering into the city, Jahziel felt very special, as if he had entered into heaven. Then, as they went into the temple area it was as if they were going into God's house, especially when Jesus began teaching the people. The last day of the feast was the most special. They had followed the priest and sang the traditional songs. When the priest poured out the water which represented the Holy Spirit, Jesus shouted out, "If anyone is thirsty, let him come to me and drink. Whoever believes in me, as scripture has said, streams of living water will flow from within him." Of course, Jesus was meaning that the Holy

Spirit would work through people who believed in Him.

The people listening to Jesus were shocked at what He said. Jahziel heard some people say that Jesus must be the Messiah. Some said, "He is a prophet," but others thought He was lying and they wanted Jesus arrested. Jahziel ran to tell Jesus that the temple guards were coming to arrest Him, but Jesus went back to teaching. When the guards came, they listened to Jesus teaching and they thought His teaching was true and wonderful, so they did not bother Him.

When night came, Jesus and Jahziel went to the Mount of Olives. This was one of Jesus' favorite places in the whole world. Upon arriving at the Mount of Olives, Jahziel felt a strange feeling come over him. It was dark, but the moon shined through the cluster of ancient weather-beaten olive trees. Within the mount was a garden called Gethsemane. There were rose bushes all around and every kind of herb grew there – oregano, parsley, thyme and mint. The aroma from the herbs made Jahziel feel peaceful. There was a scent so pure that Jahziel thought of it as the presence of God. Jahziel's mind went back to the story his father told him about the Garden of Eden before the fall and how God had walked among Adam and Eve. Jahziel thought this was a special holy place, a place where God dwells. Then Jahziel saw several tombs dug out of rock. Jahziel had never lost anyone close to him, yet, a feeling of loneliness came over him. The feeling was only momentary as the fragrant scent of the herbs brought joy to him. For a moment, Jahziel wondered how there could be both loneliness and joy in the presence of God.

Jahziel's father and the other disciples had come to the mount with the boy and Jesus. Andrew and Bartholomew and gathered twigs and started a fire and

they sang songs from the book of Psalms. Jesus taught stories late into the night.

One story most memorable was when Jesus pointed to an olive tree and said, "The olive tree is rich in beautiful blossoms that blow in the wind, scattering in all directions around the tree. Believers are like those blossoms and the tree is my Word. The believer receives the word and matures and blossoms as the spirit of Christ carries him throughout life."

Jahziel realized at that time Jesus was encouraging him to learn as much as possible about His teachings. Then, when Jahziel grew up, he could make decisions that would glorify God and bless his life and the lives of others with happiness. "We are like the blossoms of the olive tree blowing in the wind, bringing the scent of love with us wherever we go," thought Jahziel.

Jesus went on to say that the olive tree is one of God's first creations. That olive trees flourish for many years. He said, "Remember when Noah and his family with all the animals had been in the ark for many days? God gave them a sign of hope by sending a dove with an olive leaf. The olive leaf meant that nature had survived the great flood and there would be food for Noah, his family and the animals with the opportunity for a new happy life with God." Jesus told them that Christians are the hope of the world. When people are sad, Christians can come to bring peace, hope and healing.

"The soil of Israel is very rocky," Jesus continued, "making it difficult, if not impossible for many trees and other forms of vegetation to grow. The olive tree, on the other hand, thrives as it digs its roots deep down into the rocks. It's nearly impossible for the wind to blow down an olive tree. Christians are like the roots of the olive tree. The more they talk to God, the deeper their friendship grows with God. Being rooted in God strengthens us to stand up for what we believe in. When others try to blow us down with their temptations to do the wrong thing, we stand up for what is right according to God."

Jesus continued to teach on the subject of the olive tree, saying, and "The olive tree also has fruit that is delicious and nourishing. The Holy Spirit lives in us to develop God's fruit in us. Those fruits are love, joy, peace, patience, goodness, kindness, gentleness, faithfulness and self-control. While God ripens the fruit of the Spirit in us, we become more patient, kind, gentle and loving people. We look for ways to help others and to get along more peacefully."

Jesus then pointed to an olive oil press in the center of the garden and said, "Out of here flows the oil of the Spirit used to anoint, to heal, and to light our path." (Olive oil was used for many things in Israel. It was poured over the head of a person in a ceremony held to announce that they were a prophet, a priest, or a king. This was called anointing. Olive oil was also applied to the body to help to heal the body. Sometimes herbs were mixed with the oil to bring healing. Olive oil was also used to provide light from the lamps to see at night, much like the lights in our house.)

Jesus taught many things long into the night, but Jahziel grew tired as it was past his bedtime. That night the boy dreamed of the olive tree and the things Jesus taught. Jahziel thought, "When I grow up, I will be strong and learn all that I can about God so that I can help others to know God and to be strong in faith."

QUESTIONS FOR CHAPTER SEVEN

"A VISIT TO GOD'S HOUSE'

1.   How much can you remember about what went on during the Feast of Tabernacles?

2.   What did Jesus say when he pointed to the olive tree?

LESSONS FROM THE FIG TREE

CHAPTER EIGHT

Early the next morning as the cock crowed, Jahziel found himself half awake, walking back down toward Jerusalem. Jahziel was walking between his father, Shillem, and Jesus. One of the disciples asked the Master when he would set up His kingdom. Jesus told them many things that would take place first. Jahziel clearly remembered one thing he thought was most important; that the gospel must be preached in all nations before the Lord would bring about His kingdom.

Jahziel asked the Master, "What exactly is the gospel?" A big smile grew on Jesus' face. "Surely Jahziel, you might be called the least among these men, but you will become the greatest. You fulfill the words of the psalmist when he wrote, 'from the lips of children and infants you have ordained praise because of your enemies, to silence the foe and the avenger.' One day Jahziel, you will become a great evangelist who will declare my praises. Of all the things that I have said must precede the coming of the kingdom, you are the only one to ask, 'What is the gospel?' And this is the most important sign, and the mission of every believer – to preach the gospel."

"My gospel begins with the love of God. God loved His creation so much, especially the two humans He created, that He walked among them daily. Unfortunately those two humans rebelled against God and became the first to sin. Since then, everyone has sinned. Yet, God still loves everyone and everything. So, He sent me, His son, Jesus. I have never sinned and yet I will die for the forgiveness of the sin of all people. Then I will rise from the dead to give everyone who believes in me forgiveness of their sins so they can become friends with God. Believers can talk to God every day, and through the Bible and the Holy Spirit feel God's presence in their lives. That is the message that God wants everyone to know and to believe."

"Master, I will tell everyone about God's love," Jahziel said with conviction.

"Indeed you will," replied Jesus.

As the group walked along the way to Jerusalem, they passed by a fig tree. Jesus pointed to the tree and said, "There are many lessons on life that can be learned from the fig tree. For instance, when we see the leaves and the fruit beginning to appear, we know it is late spring and summer is coming. It is a symbol of new life beginning. So it is with the Kingdom of God. When all the events I have been telling you about have taken place, then you will know it is the time of the beginning of the kingdom. The rabbis have taught that the fig leaf was used in the Garden of Eden by Adam and Eve as a covering of their sin nature. But I tell you that sin cannot be covered with a fig leaf but only with the blood of a perfect lamb of God. Adam and Eve's sin was not their nakedness. God had created them that way. Their sin was disobedience of God's Word; they did not believe the truth God had taught them. They chose to believe the lie of the serpent."

"Today I give you a new teaching on the fig leaf. Just as the fig leaf is a sign of spring, summer and new life, so it reminds us of the person who comes to believe in the Son of God as their Savior. God makes us brand new and, as time goes by, He brings out fruit from us. That is not fruit that we can eat like a fig, but what is called the fruit of the Holy Spirit. He makes us more loving, joyful, peaceful, patient, kind, gentle, good, faithful and self-controlled."

"The fig tree also gives us a warning to beware of those who pretend to be believers, but in reality are false and without fruit. We learn this lesson when we see a fig tree with leaves growing, but when you get close, we find there is no fruit. In Israel a sign that the fruit of the tree is ready to eat is when the leaves are growing nicely. So it is with those who talk about being believers but are not kind, forgiving or peaceful. You must remember that God wants everyone to believe in me, Jesus, and learn to live like me. So God forgives man again and again and wants people to do better."

"I will tell you another story about the fig tree and let's see if you can understand its meaning. A man planted a fig tree in his garden and came again and again to see if he could find any fruit on it. But, he was always disappointed. Finally he told his gardener to cut it down. "I've waited three years and there hasn't been a single fig!' he said. 'Why bother with it any longer? It's taking up space we can use for something else. 'Give it one more chance,' the gardener said. 'Leave it another year and I'll give it special attention and plenty of fertilizer. If we get figs next year, fine, if not, I'll cut it down.' "

Jahziel thought for awhile, then he said, "The tree is like the believer. We are to obey God and as we do, we will grow spiritual fruit. God watches over us and continues to forgive us when we disobey. He gives us all the help we need to obey Him. And God always gives us the chance to repent."

"Yes Jahziel, you are right again. But also know this: some people, like the tree that grows leaves yet does not bare fruit, will be given many chances to believe and follow God's way, but will refuse to believe by God's terms."

"Yes Master, and that is very sad because I want everyone to believe."

"Jahziel, are you familiar with the saying of the prophet Michah when he said, 'Every man shall sit under his vine and his fig tree.' "

"No Master, I don't know that saying. What does it mean?"

"The prophet was speaking of a time when there wouldn't be any wars and everyone would live in peace and safety."

Excitedly, Jahziel spoke up, "Master, when will that happen?"

"Just as we have been discussing about the gospel when it is preached to all who will believe," Jesus replied.

"I cannot wait to sit under my own fig tree! Therefore, I will tell everyone about your gospel, Master."

"Here we are at the gate to Jerusalem. We shall go to the temple area," said Jesus. Entering into the city, Jahziel noticed a boy his age and he approached the boy. "Shalom, I am here with my Master who is Jesus, the great teacher, and we're going to the temple area where the Master will teach anyone who wants to listen. Would you like to come along? My name is Jahziel." "Shalom," said the boy, "I am here with my father and we are selling food to the pilgrims who have come to worship here in Jerusalem. Perhaps my father will let me come with you Jahziel. My name is Aaron." "Go ask", encouraged Jahziel excitedly.

Aaron ran off to talk with his father and a few minutes later Aaron came running back, shouting, "Jahziel, Jahziel, my father told me to go with you and he will try to join us later because he wants to hear the Master teach too. My father said Jesus is the one all of Israel has been waiting for!"

The two boys ran to catch up with Jesus and the disciples. As they ran along, Jahziel spotted a young girl sitting in the street with her mother selling herbs. The girl smiled at the boys as they ran by. Jahziel grabbed Aaron's arm and stopped running. He said to Aaron, "Let's invite that girl to come along with us to hear the Master teach." "Okay," Aaron replied, and the two boys went back to where the girl and her mother were sitting. "Shalom, my name is Jahziel and this is my friend Aaron. We are going to hear the Master teach. Would you like to come along?" "I would love to," said the girl, "but I must stay with my mother. She is blind and needs my help." "Blind!" exclaimed Jahziel; "All the more reason you should come and bring your mother. I am sure the Master will heal her." The girl's mother anxiously called out, "Please take my hand; lead me to Him. I know He is Jesus, the Anointed One. I believe He can heal me. He has come as the prophet said, that the blind will see and the lame shall walk. Please, please, take my hand."

Just as Jahziel and Aaron reached out to hold the woman's hand, her daughter, with great joy in her voice said, "My name is Esther and my mother is Mara." "Ah, Mara means bitter," pronounced Jahziel. "Your mother's life has been bitter because of blindness, but the Master will change her name to Naomi. For as Naomi means pleasant, so life with Jesus is pleasant."

As the boys helped Mara to her feet, Esther said, "I was named after a queen." Jahziel responded, "Yes, one who freed our people. But Jesus will free us forever." Jahziel and Esther looked at each other and smiled.

The little group hurried toward the temple where Jesus would be teaching, Jahziel and Aaron wanted to run, but they realized that Mara was blind and depended on Esther to lead her, so the boys could only go according to Mara's

speed.

As they made their way along the crowded streets, Jahziel thought to himself, "I am doing just as the Lord commanded all believers to do. I am gathering people to hear the gospel of God's kingdom. This makes me happy and I feel the peace of the Lord that Jesus spoke of when he said, 'My peace I give to you, not as the world gives, for in this world you will have troubles, but in me you will have peace.' "

When the group reached the temple area where Jesus was to teach, there was already a large crowd gathering around the Lord. When Jesus saw Jahziel and his friends, He smiled at Jahziel and nodded His head motioning for the boy and the group to approach Him.

The three children led Mara to Jesus. Jahziel proudly introduced his friends. "Master, these are my new friends, Mara, her daughter Esther, and Aaron. Mara is blind. Suddenly Mara blurted out, "Lord, say the word and I will see my daughter's face. You are the Holy One of Israel!"

Jesus looked into Mara's eyes and said, "Your name is Mara meaning bitter due to your blindness, but now I call you Naomi, meaning pleasant, because your faith has healed you." As Jesus spoke those words, He reached out and touched the woman's eyes and she could then see. The woman began joyfully shouting, "I can see my daughter's beautiful face! Praise God! Surely Jesus is the Son of God."

The people who witnessed the healing began to give praise to God. Some of them said, "Surely God has sent this Jesus to be the Savior of Israel. How else could he open the eyes of the blind, except by the power of God."

Jahziel pondered all that had happened so far at the start of this new day.

He had learned lessons about the fig tree as well as making three new friends, introducing them to Jesus and witnessing a miraculous healing. But the most important lesson was learning the meaning of the gospel and carrying out the spreading of the gospel. And to think, the day was just beginning!

QUESTIONS FOR CHAPTER EIGHT

"LESSONS FROM THE FIG TREE"

1.   What is the gospel message?

2.   Do you remember some of the things Jesus said about the fig tree?

3.   Can you recall the name of Jahziel's new friend?

4.   Who was the girl that was named after a queen?

5.   What was wrong with the girl's mother?

AARON'S FATHER GETS A NEW FOOT

CHAPTER NINE

The crowd that gathered to hear Jesus teach grew to a huge number after Mara was healed of her blindness. People seemed to be coming from every direction bringing with them friends and relatives who were sick, lame or blind. Jesus healed many that day while He also preached about eternal life and the eternal city.

Jesus spoke, "There will be a river of the water of life, as clear as crystal, flowing from the throne of God and of the Lamb down the middle of the great street of the city. On each side of the river stands the tree of life bearing twelve crops of fruit, yielding its fruit every month. And the leaves of the tree are for the healing of the nations. No longer will there be any curse. God's children will see His face, and His name will be on their foreheads. He will wipe away every tear from their eyes. There will be no more death or mourning or crying or pain. There will be no need for a lamp or the light of the sun, for the Lord will give them light. The old order of things will have passed away and they will reign with God in the eternal city forever and ever.

Jahziel sat there trying to imagine such a place. He thought that these were the most beautiful words Jesus ever spoke. In his imagination he saw himself and his family and friends sitting on some steps leading to the throne. He could look out and see the river flowing through the eternal city and the tree of life with its fruit and leaves that brought peace and healing to so many.

Meanwhile, Aaron had slipped away and ran back to get his father because Aaron wanted his father to be healed by Jesus. Aaron's father had been born with a mal-formed foot which caused him to limp when he walked. Jahziel's vision of the eternal city faded at the sounds of Aaron's voice shouting to him, "Jahziel, help my father get to Jesus." Jahziel darted out ahead running up to Jesus crying out, "Master, please, my friend's father needs a new foot."

Jesus warmly smiled at Jahziel, "Your friend's father! My Jahziel, you are certainly gathering many for the kingdom." Aaron's father fell before Jesus, "Lord, we know that you are the one that all the prophets declared would come to save Israel from our sins. I am but a simple man. Please forgive me of my sins."

"Your foot is not crippled because you sinned. Many people have physical handicaps and it's not because they sinned in a way to deserve such a problem. All people have sinned, but not all have physical handicaps. Sin affects our souls and prevents people from spending eternity with God in His kingdom. Have faith in the Son of God and you will have a place in God's kingdom forever."

"Sir, I have faith that you are God's son come to save those who believe," replied Aaron's father.

Jesus looked compassionately on the man and asked, "What is your name?"

"My name is Saul."

Then Jesus said, "Stand and walk Saul, for your faith has been heard by my Father."

Immediately, Saul stood up and walked without a limp. All the people who saw this miracle praised God and declared, "Blessed is He who comes in the name of the Lord."

While all the celebrating and praising was going on, Jahziel's father, Shillem, pulled Jahziel aside and quietly spoke to him. "Jahziel, be careful. Trouble is brewing. The leaders of the synagogue are plotting against Jesus. They are concerned for their own power. They see that the people love Jesus and want to make Him king over Israel. The leaders are afraid that they might lose their place of power and authority over the people. They have grown very wealthy by cheating the people out of their money. Jesus told me to keep you safe if anything should happen to Him.

"But father, nothing can happen to Jesus. He is the Savior."

"Jahziel, have you not been listening to what the Mater has been telling us? On one occasion He said, 'tear down this temple and in three days I will raise it up.' Peter and the others think He means the temple at Jerusalem, but I believe Jesus was referring to His body as the temple. Another time He said, 'for as Jonah was three days and three nights in the belly of a huge fish, so the Son of Man will be three days and three nights in the heart of the earth.' He also said that He must go to Jerusalem and suffer many things and be killed, and on the third day be raised to life. Even John the Baptist said, 'Behold the Lamb of God who takes away the sin of the world.' I ask you my son, how can a sacrificial lamb take away the sin of the world without dying? I tell you Jahziel; great harm will come to our Master, Jesus, but I believe God will raise Him from the dead. So, fear not my son, but believe this must happen. But, you must be kept safe because you have been chosen to tell the story to many people."

"Yes father, what you say makes sense. Now I understand that many of the things Jesus told me about are to happen after He raises from the dead. It makes me sad to think Jesus must suffer and die, but that is overshadowed by the joy of Him raising to life again. I realize that because Jesus lives, we who believe in Him will also rise up from death and live forever with God and our family and friends who also believe. It is important that we tell everyone about the gospel of Jesus!"

"Come Jahziel, draw aside with me and watch what the religious leaders will do to trap Jesus so that they can have Him arrested." Immediately after Shillem got Jahziel away from the crowd, a disturbance erupted as a teacher of the Law pushed through the crowd and came before Jesus, saying with a loud voice so everyone could hear, "Good teacher, you speak very knowledgeably of the kingdom of heaven. Almost as if you have been there! You tell how these common people will be there enjoying time with God. Well, what do you say about me? How can I inherit the kingdom of God?"

Jesus looked at the man and knew that the man was trying to get him to say something that was against the religious law so that he could have Jesus arrested. Therefore, Jesus said, "Why do you call me good? Isn't it true that only God is good and all others have sinned and are in need of a savior? So, who do you say I am?" The man just stood there silent. Then Jesus spoke, "You know the commandments. Do not commit adultery, do not murder, do not steal, and do not give false testimony, honor your father and mother."

After a moment, the man replied, "All these commandments I have kept since I was a child."

When Jesus heard him He said to the man, "There is one more thing to do to be perfect; sell everything you own and give the money to the poor and you will have your treasure in heaven. Then, come follow me."

When the man heard this he became very sad because he was very rich. Jesus looked at the man and said to all, "How hard is it for the rich to enter the kingdom of God! Indeed, it is easier for a camel to pass through the eye of a needle than for a rich man to enter the kingdom of God."

Those who heard what Jesus said asked Him, "Who then can be saved?"

Jesus replied, "What is impossible with man is possible with God." In other words, no one is capable of being perfect enough to keep all of the rules of the Law truthfully, but because God is merciful, He has sent His son who does keep the Law and who is the sacrificial lamb who takes away the sin of those who believe.

Peter then spoke up and asked, "What about us who have left all we had to follow you?"

Jesus responded lovingly, "I tell you the truth, it is you and others to come that I speak of. Anyone who leaves behind the opportunities of the world, or even has to leave their own family to travel as a missionary to serve the kingdom of God, will receive a great reward in eternal life and will enjoy a special peace in this life. Although you will miss your family and the familiar surroundings where you live, knowing you are obeying God will keep you happy and at peace."

The people who believed in Jesus all cheered and jumped for joy to know that they were loved by God and would receive eternal life because they followed Jesus. The false leaders had wrongly taught them that poor and sick people were poor and sick and were being punished by God. They were also taught that the only way they could get right with God was through making animal sacrifices and paying money to the leaders at the temple.

Jesus went on to teach more on this subject. He used the 34th chapter of Ezekiel. In that chapter, God spoke through the prophet using the example of shepherds and sheep, comparing them to leaders for not taking proper care of the people. But he also said that the common people, whom he called the sheep or the flock, need to be careful how they treat each other. Regardless of whether someone is rich or poor, God expects all people to treat each other with kindness, patience, gentleness and love.

After listening to the teachings of Jesus, the ones who were dishonest among the leaders became very angry. They did not want to change and be kind or share with the poor. They talked among themselves about stoning Jesus in order to frighten the people and keep them from following Jesus. But Nicodemus and some of the other leaders who believed Jesus told the others not to harm Jesus. And so, the leaders argued among themselves. Jesus, being aware of what was going on with the leaders, decided it would be best to leave so that no one would get hurt.

Jesus, His disciples, Jahziel, Jahziels's new friends, and Shillem all left Jerusalem. They journeyed along the road heading to Bethany, a town where Jesus had friends they could visit while enjoying some peace and quiet. As the devoted group of believers walked along the mountainous road, Jahziel walked beside his father. Shillem asked the boy, "My son, what have you learned from our time with Jesus today in the temple?"

"I have learned from Naomi and Saul that faith can heal. Father, I have also come to believe that faith in Jesus can heal more than just physical health. If everyone would put their faith in Jesus, then all the problems of the world would be healed. If we trust Jesus, there would be no reason to say bad things to others or to hate anyone or physically harm another person. No one would take up a weapon against someone else. Along with faith comes humility among the rich and the poor. Regardless of who we are, we should always put serving others above wanting our own way."

"From the reactions of the corrupt leaders, I understand that when God challenges our faith, those who are evil will grow more angry and the true believers will become more faithful. Today has been a day to learn much about faith. I wonder what lies ahead for us in the town of Bethany," Jahziel concluded.

QUESTIONS FOR CHAPTER NINE

"AARON'S FATHER GETS A NEW FOOT"

1.　　Jahziel imagined living in the eternal city. Can you do the same and tell us what you think it will be like?

2.　　What did Jahziel say he learned from his day in the temple?

TELL MY SISTER TO HELP

CHAPTER TEN

Jesus and his group of disciples made their way up and down the dusty mountain road that led eastward, out of Jerusalem toward Bethany. Jahziel, running and walking to keep up with the group, remarked to his father as he looked back, "Father, the crowd following us is as large as the crowds that gathered to see Jesus around the Sea of Galilee." "Yes son, and they are talking about making Jesus king. This kind of talk angers the leaders of the synagogue."

As the day wore on, Jahziel grew thirsty from the hot sun and dry road. The group reached the top of a hill from where they could see the town of Bethany. Drawing close, Jahziel saw the elders of the village sitting at the main gate. As was the custom in Israel, each village had a main gate where the wisest men would sit. They would be very informed in the Law and be honest and able to make wise decisions. People who had a problem with a neighbor or a family member could come to the elders at the gate for help in solving the problem.

Jahziel noticed from a distance that one of the elders stood up and ran toward the group. As the man approached the group, he could be heard shouting out, "Jesus, Master, we welcome you to our town." The elder fell before Jesus reaching out to touch Jesus' feet as if to worship the Lord. But Jesus, calling the man by name, said, "Lazarus my friend," reaching down and helping him to his feet. Then Jesus kissed Lazarus on each cheek, as was the custom between friends in that culture.

"It has been a long time since we have visited. How are your sisters Mary and Martha?" Jesus asked. "Oh, they are healthy and happy," Lazarus replied. "Martha is as busy as ever! They will be so glad to see you. I will send a runner ahead to tell them you are coming. You will stay at our house, of course." "My disciples and I will be honored to stay with you and your family," replied Jesus.

Jesus turned to the crowd that had followed them for the short distance between Jerusalem and Bethany. He explained that He and the disciples would be staying with Lazarus and his family, and that the crowd was welcome to either stay in Bethany or return home for the night.

While Jesus was speaking to the crowd, Jahziel heard a woman scream, then a man's voice shouting, "Stop thief, stop!" Jahziel, tugging on Jesus' robe nervously exclaimed, "Master, Master, there is trouble." Jesus responded immediately, reaching through the crowd. Jahziel followed behind, his heart pounding as he made his way through a maze of adults who were now moving in the same direction as Jesus. Shortly, Jahziel came upon a tense scene. The thief had been caught and some men were beating and kicking him, while others were picking up rocks to stone him. Suddenly, Jesus appeared from the crowd. He pulled the men off the thief and stood over the bleeding and beaten man. Jesus addressed the hostile crowd, "Wait! Why are you attacking this man?"

"He is a thief," the attackers exclaimed. "He has stolen money from a poor family."

Jesus stared down at the frightened thief. "Is this the truth?" Have you stolen money?"

"Yes, I need to feed my family and have not been able to find work. I have been shunned by the synagogue because I could not pay the temple tax."

Jesus looked at the crowd and asked, "What does the Law say should be done with this man?"

Several voices proclaimed the punishment, "Cut off the hand that stole!...Stone him...Drive him out of the city!"

Jesus sternly spoke, "Have you not read the prophet Zechariah? Execute true justice, show mercy and compassion, everyone to his brother." He continued, "And does not the psalmist say, 'But he, being full of compassion, forgave their iniquity, and did not destroy them. Yes, many a time he turned his anger away and did not stir up all His wrath.' "

"I hear talk among you that the tax collectors overcharge you and the synagogue leaders spend your temple tax on luxuries for themselves, yet you do not attack them or attempt to stone them. But this man who is powerless, you want to kill him. Which one of you has kept the Law perfectly? Who among you has not stolen from God by taking advantage of God's mercy? I say to you, help this man to stop stealing. Someone among you give him a job." Jesus then reached down and helped the man to his feet. The Lord quietly said to the man, "Work hard and sin no more. The grace of God has been on you today; do not tempt the Lord."

Jahziel observed some men who came and spoke with the man, offering him work. Some of the women gave him food for his family. Jahziel also overheard some of the religious leaders from Jerusalem that mingled throughout the crowd. They said, "This man Jesus interprets the Law like we have never heard before. We have expelled this man from the synagogue for not paying the temple tax and Jesus finds a way for him to support his family, and now he will be able to pay the temple tax. Why didn't we think of this? Have we been so narrow minded in our interpretation of the Law? Jesus brings out a kinder side of God; truly, He must be the Holy One of Israel, the Messiah we have waited for all these years!"

Then one of the other keepers of the Law spoke, "This man that Jesus helped is a thief and a sinner. Once a thief, always a thief. Jesus has no right helping him. Holy One of Israel?" he scoffed. "If Jesus was holy, He would have condemned the sinner. Let's go back to Jerusalem, I've seen enough of this rebel. We must make a plan to put an end to all His foolishness!"

Jahziel did not want to bother the Lord with what he overheard, so he waited until later that evening when they were alone at the home of Martha, Mary and Lazarus. Indeed, that turned out to be a very interesting night. In reply to what Jahziel told Jesus about the religious leaders, Jesus reminded Jahziel that He, Jesus, must die and rise again on the third day. He further informed the boy that although some of the leaders would believe in Jesus as Messiah, they would be overruled by those who were opposed to Him. But, Jahziel was not too worried about all of this for it was part of God's plan to take away sin and allow us to live forever in heaven with God. Jahziel was blessed to have been picked as the boy who would write the story about Jesus' life.

The same night, while visiting at the home of Jesus' friends, Martha became very upset and complained to Jesus that she was doing all the work, preparing the meal for everyone, while her sister Mary just sat around listening to Jesus teach. Martha did calm down after Jesus explained to her that He appreciated the hard work she put into the meal. He reminded her that even if they missed a meal to learn a lesson about the kingdom of God, they would be more blessed. Martha admitted that the things of heaven were even more important than a nice supper.

The next morning when the group prepared to leave, Jahziel overheard Jesus talking to Lazarus. "When I come back to Bethany, the Lord said, "the faith of this house will be tested. Pray that your faith will hold firm." Lazarus did not know at that time what the Lord meant.

Walking out of the house, they were met by a larger crowd that had been waiting for them. Jesus began calling out men's names, and as did so the men stepped out of the crowd. When Jesus had gathered seventy of them, He teamed them up two by two and gave them instructions to go into all the towns and villages ahead of Him and prepare the people for His arrival. Their message to the people was to repent, because Jesus, the Messiah, was coming to visit and to tell them about the kingdom of God. Later, when these men reported back to Jesus, Jahziel heard them say that they were able to heal the sick and had the power over evil spirits by faith in Jesus. Jesus told them that they did a good job and they should be happy because their names were written in heaven. In other words, because they believed in Jesus as their Lord and Savior, they were guaranteed by God that they would live in heaven forever and ever.

When they were getting ready to leave Bethany and head north, someone asked Jesus to give an example of what we should ask for in our daily prayers. Jesus replied, "Call God your perfect heavenly Father and tell Him you believe He is the Most Holy. Ask that His will would be done by bringing His kingdom about

in the same manner here on earth as it is in heaven. Ask for Him to provide your

daily food for you and to forgive you of the sins you commit each day. Also, ask

for help in forgiving those who do mean things. Don't let yourself be overwhelmed

by temptations but always turn to Him instead of following evil. Then Jesus shared

an example:

> "Perfect Heavenly Father, Holy One. May your kingdom come
> according to Your time and will on earth as it is in heaven.
> Provide the food we need daily. Forgive our daily sins, and
> help us to forgive others. Please don't let us fall into temptations,
> but keep us from evil. Thank you Holy and all-powerful God.
> Father, Son and Holy Spirit. Amen."

Walking with Jesus Jahziel thought about how good, kind, gentle and loving

Jesus was and how He wanted to be just like Jesus. He thought about all that he

had learned in this short time with Jesus. Jahziel also promised that he would write

the story of all other events he witnessed when he traveled with Jesus. He would

someday write about being with Jesus at Jacob's well in Sychar and hearing Jesus

give His Sermon on the Mount. Jahziel would write about witnessing the

crucifixion of Jesus and about the time he spent with Jesus after Jesus'

resurrection. He would tell of the amazing way in which Jesus ascended into

heaven. Jahziel hoped that everyone would read his stories about Jesus and would

be changed by the power and love of the Lord's gospel.

QUESTIONS FOR CHAPTER TEN

"TELL MY SISTER TO HELP"

1. Who was the elder at Bethany who ran to meet Jesus and what are the names of his sisters?

2. Tell what Jesus said it meant to have your name written in heaven.

2833572

Made in the USA